Let's Have Hot Pot!

Before You Read

The story starts in Changchun, a city in northeast China. However, the main kind of **hot pot**[1] in the story comes from Sichuan in southwest China. The capital of Sichuan is Chengdu. The story also mentions Beijing, the capital of China, and Guangdong, an area of China in the south, near Hong Kong.

Chengdu, China

A. Chinese Cooking Styles. Read the paragraph. Then complete the sentences with the correct forms of the underlined words.

> When we talk of Chinese cooking, it is important to remember that China is a large country, with different cultures and at least eight different kinds of regional foods. And while spicy food is quite popular in China, only two of the main cooking styles are really all that hot: Sichuan and Hunan food. More commonly, depending upon the area, Chinese food tastes either a little salty or sweet. Since China has such a range of different kinds of foods and ingredients, nearly everyone can find some Chinese food that they will like.

1. Jake had to drink a lot of water because he ate something that was too _____ .
2. _____ where you go in China, the most common kind of food is rice or noodles.
3. Chicken is a common _____ in Chinese meat dishes.
4. The people of Guangdong eat such a wide _____ of foods.
5. The kinds of foods that people eat can tell a lot about their _____ .
6. Many tourists visiting China are surprised because the Chinese food in China often _____ very different from the Chinese food they are used to eating back home.

[1] *hot pot: a kind of Chinese cooking method where meat and other things are cooked in a broth or in water*

B. Beijing Duck. Read the postcard and look at the photos in this reader. Then answer the questions below.

Hi Kim,

Yesterday, we arrived in Beijing, and so immediately we decided to go out to see the Great Wall. Then when we came back, we decided to try Beijing's most famous food —Beijing duck. The restaurant was quite crowded, so it felt like it took forever to find a table. But when the duck came, all the waiting was worth it. The food was amazing! It was a perfect meal to end a perfect day in China's capital. Tomorrow we fly out to Chengdu, and so maybe we can try some Sichuan hot pot!

Take care!
Bill

1. Have you tried Beijing duck? What was it like?
2. What do you know about Sichuan hot pot? Why do you think it is called "hot pot"?
3. Why do you think people in Sichuan might eat hot pot and other spicy foods?
4. Are there any other kinds of hot pot? How do you think they are different from Sichuan hot pot?

The first time I ate Sichuan hot pot was in Changchun in northeastern China, more than 2,700 kilometers from Sichuan's capital, Chengdu. I had only been in China for a week when Rui, my new Chinese friend, asked me, "Have you ever had hot pot?"

"No, what is it?" I answered.

"It's good. You'll really like it. See you tonight at 7?"

And so it was decided.

The hot pot restaurant was one of the largest and busiest places in the city. Hundreds of people were crowded into one large room, sitting at tables, each with a large pot in the middle.

Track 1

We found a table at the far end of the room. Soon a large hot pot arrived, carried by a waitress. Rui said something, and she left, only to come back minutes later carrying plates full of thin slices of lamb. The hot pot itself had two sides. In one side was a cloudy white **broth**.[2] The broth in the other side was covered with bright red oil.

> [2] **broth:** clear soup made from vegetables, fish, or meat

Infer Meaning

1. What did Rui probably tell the waitress?
2. Why do you think the hot pot had two sides, one side with a spicy broth and the other side without red peppers?

Let's Have Hot Pot! | 7

"Is that red pepper oil?" I asked.

"Yes," Rui answered. "You should try it. If you like spicy food, you'll really enjoy it."

Rui picked up a thin slice of lamb with his **chopsticks**,[3] and then put it in the red broth. In seconds, it was cooked, and he put it on my small plate.

"If it's too spicy, you can use this other broth—it's not spicy at all because it doesn't have any peppers in it." Rui pointed to the cloudy white broth on the other side of the pot.

"No," I said, "this is fine."

But it was more than fine: It was spicy, **mouth-numbing**,[4] and amazing. I ate and ate until the restaurant was almost closed. I just couldn't get enough of it.

---

[3]**chopsticks:** *two thin sticks used for eating with*
[4]**mouth-numbing:** *making your mouth less able to feel things*

For hundreds of years—and possibly much longer—millions of Chinese people have felt the same way: They just can't get enough hot pot. It has always been one of China's most popular foods.

Perhaps the most popular kind of hot pot is the Sichuan hot pot, with its spicy red peppers. What makes Sichuan hot pot different from other hot pots is the use of **huajiao**.[5] This spice is hard to describe. Depending upon who you ask, it can taste like lemons or even soap, but some people say that it really has no taste at all, and some people think it tastes bad and do not like it. This spice is mouth-numbing, and also has the strange effect of making the red peppers taste even hotter. Sichuan food is famous for its red peppers and huajiao. It is said that the spicy food helps people get through Sichuan's hot and wet weather.

[5] **huajiao:** also known as Sichuan peppercorns; a spice used in Sichuan cooking

Distinguish Facts and Opinions

1. From the passage, what facts do we know about *huajiao*?
2. What do many people think about *huajiao*?

Nearly as famous as the Sichuan hot pot is the Beijing hot pot. The Beijing hot pot uses lamb and many of the same ingredients as the Sichuan hot pot, but has a lighter taste. Since its broth is mostly just water and has no red peppers, it is not spicy. The pot itself is also different from most others. It is made of **brass**[6] and has a **chimney**[7] in the middle, and the food is cooked over a fire.

[6] **brass:** *a yellow metal*
[7] **chimney:** *a long pipe for getting smoke away from a fire*

The Northeast Chinese hot pot usually contains pork and **pickled**[8] cabbage, while the Guangdong hot pot uses a chicken or a fish broth, and is known for its wide range of ingredients, including **seafood**.[9] In fact, while lamb hot pot is quite popular, almost any kind of ingredient can be found in hot pot cooking. There are as many kinds of hot pots as there are cooks.

Today, the hot pot is one of the most popular forms of cooking in China, and nearly every village, town, and city has one—or several—hot pot restaurants. But why shouldn't hot pot be popular? With a hot pot, you can put in any ingredient that you like. The same pot can serve any number of different

> [8] **pickled:** a food that is put in vinegar or salt so that it can be kept a long time
> [9] **seafood:** food from the ocean

meals to the people sitting around the table. No one is left out, and everyone gets to eat as much—or as little—as they want. This shows the Chinese cultural values of openness and sharing. Finally, not only does hot pot taste wonderful, but eating hot pot is the perfect way to spend time with others.

In China, people like to joke that there is no problem that a hot pot can't solve. The fire from a hot pot can **melt**[10] just about any icy disagreement and warm just about any heart. Over a hot pot people can talk and share not just food, but friendship. While the food may soon be forgotten, these friendships stay with us forever. Even today, when I think of hot pot, my friend Rui's face immediately comes to mind, and I remember all the good times I spent with him.

[10] **melt:** *to change something from a solid to a liquid*

Since there are so many different ways to make hot pot, it is easy to cook hot pot in your own home using your own favorite ingredients. Even in the West, you can easily buy a Chinese hot pot broth mix from your Asian market. The only other things you really need are a large pot, a small tabletop range, and some friends to share your food with. You should try it!

What Do You Think?

1. What are some reasons hot pot might be popular in China?
2. Why is hot pot such a good place to share and build friendship?
3. Would you like to eat hot pot? If so, what kind of hot pot would you like to eat? Why?

 **After You Read**

A. **Multiple Choice.** Answer the questions below by choosing A, B, C, or D.

1. How long had the writer and Rui probably been friends when Rui asked the writer out?
   A. for a long time
   B. a week
   C. they were not yet friends
   D. forever

2. On page 4, when it says, "And so it was decided", what does "it" refer to?
   A. that the writer had never eaten hot pot
   B. seeing each other at 7 o'clock so they could talk about hot pot
   C. going out to eat hot pot at 7 that night
   D. that the writer would someday try hot pot

3. Why did the writer probably not try the cloudy white broth?
   A. He really loved spicy food.
   B. He really hated spicy food.
   C. It had red peppers in it.
   D. He was afraid to try it.

4. What does this phrase on page 14 mean: "There are as many kinds of hot pots as there are cooks"?
   A. Since there are only a few cooks, and all the cooks make the same kind of food, there are only a few kinds of hot pot.
   B. Since there are many cooks and every cook has his or her own style, there are many different kinds of hot pot.
   C. Every hot pot is different.
   D. Every cook is different.

5. What would be a good heading for the second paragraph on page 17?
   A. Hot Pots Can Melt Anything!
   B. Spice Makes Nice
   C. Forget the Food, Remember the Friendship
   D. Hot Pots Warm the Heart as Well as the Stomach

B. Complete the Notes. Complete the notes below with words from the passage.

Kinds of Hotpot

Hot pot
- Sichuan — uses (1)_____, red peppers, huajiao
- Beijing — uses lamb, has a (2)_____, no red peppers, not (3)_____
- (4)_____ Chinese — contains pork and pickled cabbage
- Guangdong — a chicken or a fish broth, a (5)_____ of ingredients, including (6)_____

C. Answer the questions. Use information from the passage to answer the questions below.

1. What does hot pot remind the writer of?
2. How can you have real Chinese hot pot?
3. What does hot pot cooking tell us about Chinese culture?
4. What other Chinese foods do you know about?

Chinese Food Culture:
More Than Just Food

🎧 Track 2

There are a few ways in which Chinese restaurants are different from Western restaurants.

Consider how Westerners go about eating at restaurants. Everyone always gets their own menu and orders their own food. And, since the tables are usually small, it is quite difficult to talk to—or even see—more than a few people during the meal.

While in modern China there are many Western-style restaurants, the traditional Chinese restaurant experience is quite different from in the West. Usually, everyone sits at large, round tables where it is easy to see and talk with each other, even if it is a rather large group. One person orders the food for everyone, after considering the likes and dislikes of the other people in the group. Then, when the food comes, all of it is put in the middle of the table. Everyone then serves themselves by taking a small bit of food and putting it on their own plates.

Just as in the West, people can choose what they want to eat. However, while in the

West, importance is placed on the individual and having one's own preferences, in China importance is placed on sharing and community. Instead of seeing themselves as individuals first, and part of the group second, Chinese people generally see themselves as part of the group first and individuals second. Everyone still gets what they want, but it is a shared experience.

Finally, since people are seated at a round table, everyone is treated equally. No one person is given greater importance over another. However, respect is still shown to older people or people of higher status, as they always sit at the far end of the room facing the door.

China has many different styles of food and a wide range of ingredients and cooking methods. And so, when you are in China, you should make an effort to enjoy Chinese food as much as possible. However, you should also make an effort to enjoy it as the Chinese do—as a group experience—a time for sharing, family, and friendship.

Word Count: 346
Time: _____

Vocabulary List

amazing *(8)*
brass *(13)*
broth *(6, 8, 13, 14, 18, 20, 21)*
cabbage *(14, 21)*
chimney *(13)*
chopsticks *(8)*
contain *(14, 21)*
culture *(2, 21, 22)*
depend upon *(2, 11)*
friendship *(17, 18, 19, 20, 23)*
forever *(3, 17, 20)*
hot pot *(2, 3, 4, 6, 11, 13, 14, 17, 18, 19, 20, 21)*
huajiao *(11, 12, 21)*
ingredient *(2, 13, 14, 18, 21, 23)*
lamb *(6, 8, 13, 14, 21)*
light *(13)*
melt *(17, 20)*
mouth-numbing *(8, 11)*
pickled *(14, 21)*
pork *(14, 21)*
pot *(4, 8, 13, 14, 18)*
range *(2, 14, 18, 23)*
seafood *(14)*
solve *(17)*
spice *(11, 20)*
spicy *(2, 3, 6, 8, 11, 13, 20)*
taste *(2, 11, 13, 17)*
value *(17)*
worth *(3)*